Firebird

Moira Andrew

Indigo Dreams Publishing

First Edition: Moira Andrew
First published in Great Britain in 2011 by:
Indigo Dreams Publishing
132 Hinckley Road
Stoney Stanton
Leicestershire
LE9 4LN

www.indigodreams.co.uk

ISBN 978-1-907401-58-9

British Library Cataloguing in Publication Data. A CIP record for this book can be obtained from the British Library.

Designed and typeset in Palatino Linotype by Indigo Dreams.

Cover design by Ronnie Goodyer at Indigo Dreams.

Author photograph by John Martin.

Printed and bound in Great Britain by Imprint Academic, Exeter.

For Fiona and Jen,
and in loving memory of Allen

For Joy
with love
& best wishes
[illegible]

May 2015

Acknowledgements

Some of the poems have been previously published in Decanto and Poetry Cornwall, also published online in Ken*Again, Poetry International and Poetry Space.
Night's Spy-glass published by kind permission of the organisers of The Welsh Poetry Competition 2011.

Previous Poetry Publications

Light the Blue Touch Paper, Iron Press, 1986 & 1989
Fresh out of Dragonflies, Headlock, 1995
This Year, Next Year, Marvin Katz Press, 2004 & 2008

Books for teachers

Language in Colour, 1989
Words with Wings, 1991
Rainbow Year, 1994
Paint a Poem, 1996
Legend into Language, 1998
Patchwork of Poems, 2000
Tell me a Tale, 2002

Children's poems have appeared in anthologies by OUP, Collins, Scholastic, Macmillan, Ginn etc.

Fiction

The Dream Thing, Palores Publications, 2010 (a novel for teenagers)

Moira has been published by the BBC (for the schools' programmes) and has featured on Poetry Please and Something Understood by the World Service.

CONTENTS

Firebird

Calling The Tune

when I was young,
I used to throw myself
into your cold arms
rain or shine …

I'd roll my tongue
around the taste of you
relishing your lips, foam-
wet, on mine …

one whiff of your
salty pheromones and
I'd race, almost naked,
into your embrace …

once you tempted me
with a sunlit come-on,
before bearing down,
murder in your eyes …

but I forgave you … now
I no longer beat my wings
like a butterfly … I'm content
to stroll at your side …

mesmerised by the changing
colours of your coat, silver,
indigo, the purple of
ripe aubergines …

lured on by your rich
tenor, insistent, unceasing,
push-pull, push-pull …
as ever, you call the tune …

Addressing A Life

I'm not known as a numbers person,
arithmetic has largely passed me by,
yet mention 265 and I'm in the hall
of a tall red sandstone terrace, stained
glass reflections making lozenges of
colour on the floor, my Dad's bronze
plaque on the front gate. Security.

Next 88, a cramped one-room flat,
a baby girl, a rocking horse, a bunch
of anemones, rich with April brilliance.
1587, high ceilings, an open fire
glowing in the kitchen, bedtime stories,
the sound of rattling trams, the shock
of stumbling on a stolen kiss. Betrayal.

32, going upmarket, a modern semi,
one purple wall, one navy blue, all
very with-it, juggling work and home,
ironing school uniforms twice a week.
Slammed doors, divorce. 14, mid-terrace,
knickers on the line, sizes 10, 12, 14, a mixed
bag of lovers, college-life. Independence.

34, a bungalow, with the highs and lows
of solitary times, of work, of meeting men –
then, when I least expected it – *the* man.
Briefly, 95, end-of-terrace, then 76, detached,
sunlit, all the joy of mature love and passion.
A sudden death, loss. Now 19, another bungalow,
a terraced garden, a Siamese cat. Compromise.

Maybe I'm not so bad with numbers, after all.

Living The Day

Cracked ice of morning,
birds unzipping the day,
          dreams in flight.

Craving coffee, black
and strong, toast, a shower's
          pinpricks on skin.

Ghost footsteps die away,
routine takes over, mug,
          plates rinsed clean.

The cat, surrogate mate,
deigns to lap-sit, yawns, spruces
          up her image.

What now? Diary dates
diminish. Only photographs
          tell it as it was.

Max out the hours, fill to
overflowing with silent words,
          emails, poems.

Make soup, chopping onions
into diamonds, ribboning
          carrots and leeks.

Cut a closed camellia bud,
watch its petals unfold, making
          love to the sun.

Listen to blackbirds spinning
songs among the leaves.
          Time dawdles.

At last, the sky bronzes, cat
purrs, birds quieten, ghosts
        unbutton their coats.

Lexicon

It's not simply the whole new language
you have to learn, the I for we, not us
but me. Immediately your senses go *awol,*
no rasp of beard on your skin, no click
of a key in the lock, no shrugged-off shirt
in a heap in the corner.

Unable to undo the top, you used to pass
the Toilet Duck over to him. 'What will
I do if you go and die?' Easy answer,
complete with that smile, 'Get another
man.' Unlikely. 'Or use the pliers.'
Your solution so far.

You teach yourself to do without the broad
hand over yours on the handle of the shopping
trolley, the door being opened as soon as
your car turns in, the bedtime kiss. Even
his smell – nutty, sweaty, sweet – no longer
lurks on the other pillow.

The trouble is you have no training for
this new-found life. It's thrust upon you
between one day and the next. No time to
revise, no excuses allowed, more *Open your
paper and begin.* You wake up a wife,
go to bed a widow.

Wilderness

It's the space that does it,
the silence, a sudden sound,
        a knocking
        in the dark.

It's the day's slow tempo,
its blandness, the bleached air,
        like grass after
        too much sun.

Change flaps its butterfly
wings, catches the throat
        in an agony
        of patchwork.

The paraphernalia of life
is no more than clutter
        and less useful,
        a wilderness.

Is there a place still for me?
Only you would know,
        but you have
        lost your tongue.

Rowan Tree, St Fagans

I pretend I haven't noticed,
not yet, not yet. It's
only July, after all, under
a fevered sun.

Out of the corner of my eye,
the merest hint of colour.
Impossible. It's summer,
high summer.

Behind my back, berries slide
from gold to victorious red,
a hard winter?
an omen?

What's the point? I'm immune
to the future, to the shape
of things to come,
to bugaboos.

'Don't look,' you used to say,
knowing how my heart sank
at the very threat
of autumn.

Firebird

If my love were a bird, I reckon
a phoenix would be the best bet.
Not that he'd agree, of course, what
with that red-gold crest, that azure
tail … too loud, too gaudy,
not at all the accountant's image …
he might just approve the mulberry chest
feathers, the colour of his out-to-dinner shirt.

I've considered a range of garden birds
and discounted most of them … after all,
the garden wasn't his thing.
He was up for a bit of lawn-
mowing, but the rest was
down to me. So if my love were
a bird, he wouldn't be a blackbird or a robin.
And blue-tits are out … peanuts made him choke.

Given the choice, I expect he'd go for
a hawk, king of the skies … or a peregrine.
He'd be OK for speed … in his day
he'd been a demon right wing
on the hockey pitch. But once again
his eyes would let him down. He always
wanted to be a navigator, but spectacles were
a no-no. He never quite forgave the RAF for that.

Now – if my love were a phoenix, even
the white heat of the crematorium wouldn't
faze him. He'd rise from the flames
in a blaze of colour, living on air, immortal.
Being Welsh, he'd enjoy singing hymns
to the sun … and he'd be young and strong again …
too young, too strong for me … I'm old enough to
wear purple … he'd want to spread his wings and fly.

Sunrise

An early morning knock, cold damp darkness.
We shiver in a queue for the check-in desk –
a long wait under blue florescent lights. We
buy morning papers, sweets, bottled water.

Herded like cattle, we make our slow way
to the plane, board, belt-up, wait again.
The aircraft lumbers along the runway,
a ferocious beast barely held in check.

With a full-throated roar, it takes off, making
a brief Lilliput-land of roads and roofs below.
Cars, bug-eyed fireflies, shimmer on motorways.
As we climb into cloud, our landmarks disappear.

A thread of light stitches the cloud's grey hem,
pale yellow, almost invisible at first. It grows,
glows topaz, bronze, gold. Then, a fringe of flame,
fiery as a dragon's throat, crimson, ruby-red.

The plane enters hell's open mouth. We are
gulped down by glory, consumed by brilliance,
blinded by the glare as it flares across the clouds.
The engines are easy now, thrumming, murmuring.

Unperturbed, serene, the sun glides into morning
skies, putting on a magnificent show – for us alone,
it seems. We know it's an every-day performance,
just we're not usually around to see it happening.

Only Connect

Simply connect blackbird to air, cat
to creature comforts, child to dreams,
mouse to email, raindrops to ragwort.

Add stones, stones doubling and re-
doubling in water, their colours clear
and vivid. Stones, clay, earth, death.

Take sunshine – key to the next hill,
to the green of summer. Bud to leaf,
leaf to branch, branch to open sky.

Connect sky to shore, a thin blue
ribbon their only point of contact,
the wind of change their messenger.

Join cloud to sand, a fringe of cloud
to angels' wings, the trickle of hot
golden sand to the fingers of a baby.

Like the elements, words connect –
thought to poem, image to empty
page, human drama to literature.

Think of Shakespeare, dead these five
hundred years, our sole connection
neat black print on white paper – oh,

and that po-faced pen-&-ink portrait.

'Apeldoorn'

silent clocks   they
open baby-mouths
to the sun   keep
    their curves under wraps
        bend bonnet-heads
            on slim
                green stalks

don't be taken in –
their modesty hides
cat-yellow eyes   black
    stamens crying out for sex
        selling pollen-soot
            to up-and-
                at-'em bees

when rain tiptoes across
the grass   and birds shut
up shop for the night
    they close phallic buds
        daring the stars
            to impregnate
                their dreams

indoors   tulips loose
their purse-strings   petals
dipped in blood draw 'O's
    on white walls   take
        mortality in their stride
            die with dignity
                falling   falling

Winter's Parting Shot

a door closing on the splintering sun
the sun listening for rags of song

a snowdrop lifting skirts to morning
the morning trying on silks for size

a daffodil spear pinpricking the earth
the earth a chest of pirate treasure

a stone hunkered down in the cold
the cold filling its suitcase with sparrows

a tree exposing x-ray ribs to the skyline
the skyline focusing on shades of red

a shadow leaning elbows on the hill
the hill hugger-muggered in old leaves

a bird throwing wings and songs to the air
the air tickling the senses with feathers

a bug streaking naked across the lake
the lake stealing time from idle ducks

a stream on its blind date with the sea
the sea swallowing a mouthful of sun

Out Of Season

Nothing, absolutely nothing, can be said
in favour of today. True, it's Saturday,
but that's about all. A leaking sky, bleak
as last night's dream.

Frogs aren't up and purring yet, in these
limbo days between Christmas and spring
and every last bird has disappeared into
its darkened bolt-hole.

At two in the afternoon, no-one moves,
cars stand idle in driveways, telephones are
silent. The central heating murmurs and cats
perfect their sleeping skills.

In the leaden garden, a jarring flag of colour
as an Oriental poppy unfolds its scarlet secret.
I pad outside with scissors. No clock-watcher,
it opens defiant paper petals

and lifts the face of this black winter's day.

Priorities

(For John & Carol)

The thing is, we all have
our different priorities.
I walk into the stone-hot
afternoon, looking urgently
for your tree, your poem.

The tree I find blistering
in the heat. Gasping,
I search for carved words
in the long grass, among
spindly meadow flowers.

I discover the poem, almost
illegible, under a mat of
weeds. Sweat prickling my
eyes, I dust it off, mouth
its now unfamiliar rhythms.

They mutter that the pitiful
pink flowers are *not* weeds.
Like I said, we all have our
priorities, mine are words,
theirs the *spiny rest-harrow.*

Portrait Of A Man On Holiday

The sun makes a mirror
  of the page, blinding the reader.
He concentrates, breath shallow
  as a ghost-whisper. He wears
a striped shirt, open at the neck,
  rimless spectacles, sweat.
His head is a peeled chestnut,
  fringe of hair fine as spiderwebs,
each strand gleaming. I reach out
  to touch, one finger's worth.
He looks up smiling, lays
  a warm wide hand on my back.

Night Song

Radio 4 says nightingales
are in danger – surely they've
got that wrong?
I remember its scalpel song
slicing the summer night,
of Laveyssière.

I remember the wide bed,
how it complained as we
rolled helpless
into the middle, feeling for
one another in a spiral of
luminous dark.

I remember your grim joke,
determined grimace, when pain
twisted your heart,
me thinking how temperamental
mobiles could be in this
godforsaken valley.

But this time round your spray
worked its magic and we made
frantic love
while from deep in the patch-
work woods, rose an unbroken
thread of song.

Introduction

My toes twitch. I want to dance –
wrong time, wrong place – and
I'm not much of a dancer.
It's those two precious words,
my wife, the way he struggles
to sit up straight, the formality,
his navy M&S pyjamas morphing
into business suit and tie.

He thinks he's going to die.
I think he's going to die.
The medics give him 50:50,
Dr Penny, I'd like you to meet
my wife, he says. I shake hands
with a short bespectacled man
in a white coat, murmur a greeting.
My husband manages a smile.

Dr Penny riffles through
a sheaf of notes, nods, moves
on to the next bed. I unwrap
ham sandwiches, in triangles,
crusts cut off, unearth letters,
paperbacks, a jar of raspberries
dusted in sugar. My lover watches,
eyes pale, skin taut, transparent.

The bell rings. He reaches out
to kiss me on the mouth, squeezes
my hand. I cram dirty washing
into my bag, walk out of the ward,
the words *my wife* making music
in my head. I try not to skip, hope
no-one notices my dancing shoes
in brightest apple-blossom pink.

Birthday Gamble

Of course, they were very young
and there was the baby, crying
chuckling crazy 24-hour baby –
and the well-worn clothes (except
for the child's) and living
with hand-me-down furniture all
boxed together in a single room.

29th April, her birthday, barely
a bus fare between them, end-
of-the-month lentil soup time
and he brought home a box,
a ribbon-capped shining box
and a bunch of anemones
for the baby to give.

The baby wanted to eat them
so they traded flowers for
rusks and still the box, like
Pandora's, unopened in her hands.
'Go on,' he said. White lace
foamed and bubbled across green
candlewick, not of their choosing.

'But how?' 'The office sweep,'
he said. 'The National – I put
a quid on the beast and it won!'
The baby drummed heels on her chair.
They fed her bread and soup as
white frills spilled, by chance,
over sooty-eyed anemones.

Persephone's Daughters

They live their own lives, these
daughters. They must. OK, so
their spring was yours, but you
had to let them go – to fall out
of trees, off wobbling bicycles.

Skinned knees made better
with a kiss, a Band-Aid, a toffee –
easy it was, in those snowdrop days.
Turn your back and spring's become
summer, celandines are sunflowers.

And you, in your copper-leaved coat
must remain silent as they fall in and
out of love, their tears tearing holes in
your eyes. No pomegranates for them –
they take knives to unripe lemons.

When the autumn sun rides high,
you gather the scattered pips, poke them
into pots on the greenhouse shelf. You
pour wine, make cups of scalding coffee
and look forward to the white of winter.

Letter To My Son

Dear Martin, you'd be almost 50
by now, brother to two big sisters.
But you weren't to be … you
morphed into a clot of blood.

I remember the sun polishing
the taps on our deep sink, the
narrow lane at the back of the flats,
bikes abandoned against the wall

… and the seep of blood trickling
down my thighs. I remember
thinking how you'd never play rugby,
never mess around with boy stuff.

I fought against tears. The doctor said,
Not to worry, nature's got it right,
You don't want a damaged baby, do
you? I didn't. But I wanted you.

So Martin, you went down the loo.
Sometimes I smell you, feel the rasp
of beard on my cheek. (To tell the truth,
I haven't thought about you for years.)

Today, I remember the baby boy that
never was. Just as in those long-ago
days, the sun is shining, new taps glitter,
the lane's a field, bikes are tractors …

and I'm the mother of daughters.

In My Element

Like girls running in the wind,
hair ribboning behind them,
I swam, splashed, immersed
myself in the sea, mermaid-
style, come sun, come rain.

My mother, towel opened
wide as a gull's wings,
waited on the shore, 'Come
in !' she'd call. 'At once, d'you
hear?' I pretended not to.

She paraded the water's edge,
dodging bleak grey waves.
'You'll catch your death!'
I was in my element, diving,
ducking, floating, frothing.

In my own good time I'd
tiptoe up the shingle, shivering
now, bone-white with cold,
an alien. 'Chittery-bite?' she'd
offer, wrapping me up tight.

The towel was harsh with
sand, the tea biscuit dry and
crumbly. Out of her element,
my mother rubbed me down
in brisk uncomprehending love.

Ben The Room

I dreamed the diamond shape, the white glass
          and couldn't place it,
familiar, so familiar my fingers remembered the feel –
          and somehow, I knew to turn it upside down.

It niggled … not the caster sugar shaker, that had a silver lid –
Gran was proud of it, kept it on a high shelf, out of the steam –
not the tea-strainer – I never liked tea, not then, not now.

The dream faded, like dreams do, but still my hand
          doodled with the unresolved conundrum …
                    turned it over and over.

It melted into a Camp coffee bottle with square shoulders
and I remembered my mother's mid-morning routine, the
wobbly pan, the hissing gas, the sickly smell
                    of hot milk, a teaspoon
          of sticky brown liquid stirred in, the oomph
          as she flopped down into a comfy chair,
                    cup of so-called coffee
                              within easy reach.

And high tea – we used to sit down to high tea at six o'clock
if my dad got home in time, bread and butter, mince and potatoes,
          fish when Cousin Anne came to call.

At Gran's house, meals were taken *ben the room*, long table,
white cloth, Grandpa in pride of place, sprinkling pepper
on his strawberries, piling salt in neat white heaps at the edge
          of his meat and two veg – that's it,
          that's what my fingertips dreamed –
                    Gran's cut-glass salt cellar and its pepper-mate
                              lording it over the knives and forks
                                        and blue-rimmed china plates.

Playing Away From Home

We were packed off to our grandparents without warning –
but then, it wasn't done to explain to children in those days,
not that we'd have understood, of course.
And there were the telephone calls, the whispering
in the hall, the long faces, short tempers.

My mother disappeared, *Gone to see your Dad*, we were told.
A good-looking man, such an odd comment, picked up when
grown-ups thought we weren't listening.
Indeed he was a good-looking man, especially in wartime
RAF officer's uniform, neat moustache.

He toured the South coast in a mobile surgery, (not a Spitfire),
still a dentist, still just this side of forty, still randy, no doubt –
even now it's difficult to think of your father
being randy – surrounded, as he was, by pretty blond WAAFs,
the Bunnies and Flopsies, gagging for it, I expect.

My mother was away for a long time, it seemed to us, (probably
about four weeks all told) while we caught the tram to school,
did our homework, scurried into the shelter
most nights. She came home tight-lipped, even more of a dragon.
Dad's playing-away remained her secret weapon.

The Jam Jar

We lean our bikes against the wall,
sit in the sun, hair sweaty to the roots,
faces flushed with heat.
                                        Summer, full
of days, opens its portfolio – blank,
white, gleaming – anything is possible.

We share a bottle of warm pop, ease
skirts to our thighs, spread our legs, loll
daydreaming. Sex is a closed book,
boys a different breed. *Wonder what*
kissing's really like? Maeve sucks the back
of her hand, testing. *Must be more to it*
than this!
                    I get up, rub a peep-hole
in the dusty window, breathe on it, peer
inside the abandoned cottage. A table set
for one, spoon, knife, fork – and a jam jar
filled with dead flowers.
                                        We push open
the door, *Anyone home?* Obviously not –
detritus of years strewn, like mulch, across
the floor, grimy jam jar trapping the sun,
flowers crumbling in our fingers.
                                                    I run
outside and fill the jar at the water-butt.
We take our time, search for wild
flowers – blue, pink, white – whose names
we don't know, stuff them in the jar,
replace it on the table.
                                        Conversation stilled,
we walk our bikes back down the lane,
Maeve and me, into the heat-drenched day.

Searching For The Second Magpie

Maple branches sing into green
and one bird of joy, flaunting its
zebra feathers, zips to the place
where tree meets sky.

Not a great omen – so what's
new? You've learned to live with
the oneness of things, one plate,
one mug, one glass.

You turn from the window, shrug,
That old wives' tale! – but your
eyes strain for a flash of matching
jet-bright wings.

Your ring catches the sun – with
a sorcerer's timing, the perfect pair
strut across the grass, splendid in
full evening dress.

Kleptomaniacs, these two – gold has
done the trick. If only it were as easy
to conjure up the one person who
could change your life.

(poem title taken from a piece of music heard at Bishopgate Hall)

The Birds

'I watch … the birds,' she says,
her voice a mere feather of itself.
A heartless sun bathes her in gold.

She has been dozing, teeth fallen
from her gums to make a skull's
head of the once-familiar face.

'Doves?' I ask. They sit in a row,
punctuating next door's roof ridge.
'Birds … they're birds. I watch them.'

She is tightly packaged into a
narrow space, bed, wash basin,
chair, walking frame, commode.

'What have you been … up to?'
she asks. I fill in mundane details
of life in a half-forgotten world.

She tries to focus, drawn instead
to the comings and goings outside
her window. Birds jostle and shove.

'I watch their … antics,' she says.
A mug of tea, too hot to drink,
is put on her tray. She pushes it away.

Leaning forward, she shivers with
excitement, counting on her fingers,
'eight, nine … ten birds!' Joy – of a kind.

Chef's Secret

No kitchen whites, no frenzy,
no serving bell, just a man
in a red sweatshirt, white hair
shower-neat, a thin thread
of cigarette smoke needling
the busy morning street.
Oscar lay at his feet.

We traded small-talk. Then
I tried to prise a recipe
from him. His tomato soup
was out of this world, thick,
rich, Chianti-red. 'No secret,'
he said. 'You need tomatoes,
tomatoes and more tomatoes.'

'But there must be more to it
than that,' I persisted. The dog
stirred, looking up. André's
soft Italian burr became
more pronounced. 'Just use
enoff tomatoes,' he said.
'I'll sort out a recipe next time.'

There was no next time.
The bell was stilled, kitchen
clamour silenced. The chef's
secret was safe. But he lives on.
When I make soup, I hear
simmering echoes of his voice,
'Just use *enoff* tomatoes.'

Old Mother Goose

(In memory of Merryn)

She stands by the open window,
shaking her duvet, feathers flying.

Mesmerised by the vicious white
ballet she's created, she pushes her

glasses into place, gives the quilt
one last go. The waiting world shivers,

the sky turns black, people shrug
deep into padded anoraks, pull

woollen hats over their ears and
dig out their fur-lined boots.

From her eyrie, Old Mother Goose
plans her attack. It excites her.

She takes time to select her victim,
not the lad on the tea-tray sledge,

not the bloke peering from his yellow
gritter, not the old dear slipping on ice –

she's damaged a hip, no problem –
just the kind of thing that happens

to pensioners. No, with cool deliberation,
she chooses a woman in her forties,

driving home, Christmas presents
stowed in the boot of her car.

Her mother takes the call, answering
in her bird-like voice, *Angie here!*

The accident makes front page news,
it's all over the local TV. Gloating,

Mother Goose rubs her hands, *Job done!*
She preens before the mirror. It cracks like ice.

Five Tulips

I'd like some flowers please, I said,
eyeing up roses, alstroemeria, yellow lilies …
Sorry, the woman smiled,
        you've got to order them.
But my daughter's just died …
Sorry, she said again,
        looking past me as people do
        when it's clear they couldn't care less.

The garden centre, I thought,
but it was shut, padlocked.
        I rang the bell,
        rattled the gate.
A man shambled out, Can't you read?

I was angry, fists balled, nails biting
        into my flesh.
My daughter had died and
        I couldn't find flowers.
                I checked my vases,
nothing doing, the leaves had gone brittle,
        stems slimy, heads drooping.

A neighbour took pity on me.
        Jump in the car, he said,
        I'll pick some from my garden.
But the flowers had prickly stems,
        more bush than bouquet.
I couldn't give these to my daughter.

In the shop, the woman laid five tulips
on the counter. They were beautiful,
        mixed colours, like in a catalogue.
But they're spoken for, she said.

So I stole them, snatched them up and ran.
I wrapped the tulips in blue paper,
placing them with such precision
that each head looked its best …
yellow, pink, orange, flame-red, white …
perfect, in fact, just the flowers
for my dead daughter.

Ringing Out

Already the leaves are rimmed
with red … soon winter will steal them
from the trees and the drama
of bare branches blacken
the skyline.

I tried to call you, but
there was no answer.

There's blood on the horizon,
the crimson of berries, hawthorn,
rose hips, brambles … and thumb-tack
stars have been hammered deep
into the night.

Maybe you've changed
numbers, or did I forget?

The year is looking out
its fleecy boots and fur-lined gloves …
when owl-talk tears the silence,
I'll seek the silver of your breath
across my pillow.

You're not seeing another
woman, are you?

True, my eyes aren't as good
as they used to be … but did I see
you link arms with autumn and
go walkabout over the white
wall of winter?

'The number you called
has not been recognised.'

Catching Sunlight

Catch sunlight in your fingers,
see-through images of bird-bones,
bones caught in the chirping notes
of sparrows. Like fragments of
brittle leaves, brown birds swing
on the air. Catching the breeze,
catching a song, catching up
with time, its hours, its minutes,
slivers of errant time.

Time to breathe, time to smile,
time to die. Time is at a standstill
and stillness is everything. It catches
the moment – listening, imagining,
letting go, allowing colour to seep
into your soul. One burning question,
when we die, is colour bleached out?
No reds, no blues, no greens? A
grey existence, grey on grey?

Try catching grey in your hands,
smoke-grey, pearl-grey, mist-grey,
the grey of grandmother's hair,
the grey of my lover's eyes,
the soft grey of twilight. An
under-rated colour, nondescript,
neither crisp white, nor black,
an escapee. It's a butter-fingered
task. Catch grey – if you can.

Rehearsal

In rehearsal
I met death
on a wide
white road

where dust like
powdered bone
camouflaged
each hedge

and pallid
linen fields
bandaged
the highway.

Pumped tight
as an arm cuff,
the silence
was immense.

Colourless
blood seeped
out, pale as
dry white wine.

Nearby sprawled
a star of cars,
mortal collage
under lights

whirligigging
blue agonies
into the heat.
In real-time

the day is green
with summer.
Only the May
cascades like

white water
as I drive
unshadowed
into the sun.

Candlelight

You come to look for me,
anxious,
your dressing-gown flapping.

A summer night,
see-through dark,
Shasta daisies smiling moon-smiles,
geraniums velvet-black,
a fat candle on the garden table,
its flame tearing ragged holes
in the stillness.

Uncurious, accepting,
you sit beside me
on the slatted wooden chair,
(hard on a backside clad in pyjama bottoms).
take my hand,
twirling its wedding ring
round and round.

The silence is peppered
with small sounds,
stems creaking,
a shuffle of slippers,
the candle spluttering,
a petal falling.

The cat pads outside,
jumps on your knee.

Stocks, nicotianas, lavender,
roses hanging from the archway
trail love-letter scents across
the night air.

The flame sends a shiver
into the dark, gutters
to death's door and blackness
is absolute. I shiver too.

Storm Warning

Take down the moon,
there's a storm brewing.
Too late, look at the way
a monster broom sweeps
    across the sky.

The house huddles into
itself, trees hunker down,
but the moon sails heedlessly
on, ignoring all Met Office
    red alerts.

She shakes her feathers,
does Old Mother Moon,
outlining her crescent
with silver lipstick, with
    jet-black eyeliner.

We wait. Rain overflows
its deepest buckets and
the wind inflates its lungs
to bursting point. The moon
    shrugs, unimpressed.

'Bring me my mirror,' she
calls as clouds clamour
to do her bidding. She smirks
in satisfaction, wraps herself
    in invisibility.

But, not to worry, she'll
re-appear in her own good
time, in full stage make-up,
acknowledged glamour-puss
    of the night.

Night's Spy-glass

On the edge of silence, night
does her own thing, peers down
from a thousand quicksilver eyes,
finding us, snug as sardines,
in our wide double bed.

She can't be doing with our
lazy innocence, our looking-forward
to years of togetherness, snaps
imperious fingers, calls for
ever-stronger lenses, magnifies

a heart-problem here, a dodgy
knee there, pulling the rug
from under our complacency.
She shows her teeth, conjures
chaos music from overhead wires,

gives black-bud trees dancing
shoes, sits back and screws
a spy-glass into every star. She
sticks pins into each tender part,
Try this on for size, she says,

watching our every move
with clinical detachment. It
takes all our energy not to cry out,
simply to stroke the other's
skin and live until morning.

The Box

She found boxes fascinating –
the not-knowing, the inevitable
guessing-game.
But this box was different –
round, decorated in fancy gold-
leaf, menacing.

She'd found it hidden away
in the zipped-up pocket of his
golf-bag.
She knew, of course, he'd
been playing away from home –
wives do.

The tiny heart-shaped catch
resisted. She teased it open with
her fingernails.
Inside, cushioned in velvet, a pair
of gold earrings – he'd always had
excellent taste.

Quite beautiful, but designed for
pierced ears – something she'd never
got around to.
She removed one earring from its
deep black nest, fondled it, admiring
its delicacy.

Then she took aim, threw the pretty
thing into a field of corn. It glittered
in the sun.
She returned the box to its hiding
place. The missing earring was never
mentioned, not once.

Keepsake

She kept it to herself, not letting on, storing
memories against the rainy day that would
surely come. And come, it did.

It was the smell mostly, raw sex is like
butchery, great in its place, unpleasant if
you're not involved. She was.

And the sounds from an everyday world
seeping through the window, lawn mowers,
the click of bowls, neighbours.

They should have been somewhere else,
both of them, in a school perhaps, properly
clothed, not naked and sweaty.

No I love yous, of course – it wasn't like
that, she divorced, he between wives. It was
easy camaraderie, greedy lust.

In her bed, glowing in the aftermath, they lazed
mute in afternoon sunlight, she thinking, I'll
remember this, every last detail.

Stubble had rubbed her cheek, she remembered –
this late in the day his chin was dark with bristle –
so he stroked the place, kissed it.

He checked his watch. Time's up, he said, as usual.
They chatted amiably as they dressed. Ready to
face the mob? Your car or mine?

She hid their secret, not admitting, even to herself,
that it'd turn up in a poem one day. Not that it matters
now – the grapevine says he's dead.

Once Upon A Lifetime

'We had our good times, didn't we?'
He looked down at her, *'Didn't we!'*
Affirmation, not a question, grey eyes
set among wrinkles, hair dusted
with age, otherwise, much the same.
An elderly couple, in funereal black.

They shared histories, sipping cold
G&Ts, laughter in the background.
'We like Florida, ever been there?'
'France was more our bag, the Loire,
down to Sarlat occasionally, staying
in gites, strolling round markets … '

The actual words weren't important.
They dare not mention memories of
skin on skin, hand searching for hand
beneath the dinner table, the quickstep
excuse for feeling thigh on thigh,
breast against chest, pickpocket kisses.

It was enough to know that they both
remembered – like the time, under the stars,
when he explained port and starboard –
'A lifetime ago,' he smiled. He reached
for her hand, held it briefly, kissed her,
said goodbye. The flame was still alight.

Threesome

She sits between them, first
husband, second husband –
stilted conversation. She
barely recognises the father
of her children, thinning hair,
            thickening waistline.

No doubt she's a stranger
too, older, faded, far from
the girl he'd lusted after
before the Beatles' first LP. Second
husband observes the niceties,
            'Drink?' he asks.

Daughter's wedding – they must
be civilised. They search for
safe topics. Holidays. 'Majorca,'
says Number One, biting off
the word, 'Remember?' 'France,'
            says Number Two.

Toe-curling stuff. Somehow her
incompetence in the kitchen comes
up. A point of agreement, 'But
you should taste her soup. Nothing
to touch it!' It's a face-off. 'I know,
            I've been there.'

She reaches for her coat. 'See
you sometime?' A kiss is out,
so she settles for a touch on his
arm, goes home with the man
she loves – clicking the door shut,
            second-time-round.

The Painted Box

You lifted the lid,
let me look in,
and I liked what I saw,

the subtle colours, grey
of eyes, red of Merlot,
perfect yellow freesias,

the hints of a future,
candle-lit tables, days of mist,
days of rain, sunshine,

glimpses of permanence,
your email address, the
sound of your voice,

always Pat and Allen,
transparent in memory,
as part of the package,

but, you kept a lock
on the box, didn't let me
handle it very often,

so we didn't get around
to the business of sex
at which I excel,

though I say it myself,
as shouldn't – I don't
just write a good game,

so, close the box with
a butterfly touch, my
words are trapped inside.

Rainbow Fish

I'd no idea you had a fish
of your very own. I just opened
the *Observer* and there it was,
Allen's rainbow fish, complete
with photograph.

They are found in shallow
water, these fish, *less than*
a metre deep. Good news, I
expect – you were never much
of a swimmer.

From the Wetlands of New
Guinea, it swam off the page
and into my eyes, all 11 cm. of it,
zig-zag ribbons of colour swirling
like kite-tails.

There now, I slept with a man
who has a fish named after him –
it darts and flashes across the river
of my head, showing off iridescent
designer scales.

Sister Elizabeth's Rose

We were new to all this, knowing
nothing about religious retreats –
or Cistercian nuns, come to that,
so we hadn't a clue about
what to expect.

Open to the elements, the abbey
was perched on the top of a hill.
A note on the main door told us
to ring and enter. The bare hall
smelled of polish.

A stark notice about prayers.
Five times a day, every day,
beginning at the bleak hour
of 3.30am when the spirit
is at its peak.

From the shadows, a tall nun
emerged, her long grey skirts
whispering as she walked. We
asked to see Sister Elizabeth –
'If that's possible?'

'Who shall I say is calling?'
Now this posed a problem.
'It's a present,' we said. 'From
a friend in France,' showing her
the rose in its pot.

Sister Elizabeth, plump as
a dumpling, cradled the rose
stroking its crumpled pink petals.
She looked bewildered, saying,
'I never get visitors.'

They served us coffee in the
gloom of their Spartan parlour,
wooden table, upright chairs,
an intimidating cross hanging
high on the wall.

They showed us photographs,
talked about coming to terms
with email. Ordinary women,
ordinary conversation, bizarre
circumstances.

Following in Sister Elizabeth's
wake, we trailed across beaded
grass to the garden she had dug
out of the hillside. 'Sometimes
I have to get out.'

But she'll never get out. A
neat graveyard waits at the back.
She was almost late for prayers.
'Look at the time,' she gasped, lifting
her skirts and running.

The Old Lady In The Blue Sunhat

Sometimes she wanted to scream.
In fact, she wanted to scream
a lot of the time.

But things, people,
got in the way. Everyone
expected better of her. So
she learned to keep schtum.

Sometimes the smallest details
sabotaged her best efforts.

It might be birdsong, snow
embroidering winter trees, coming
across his handwriting on labels
and the backs of photographs.

Once it was a list, found
in the depths of a jacket pocket,
wine, butter, grapefruit, cat food ...

Today, high summer,
it was the extravagance of poppies
that nearly did for her,
florid orange-red petals
smouldering in the sunshine.

And inside, the inconceivable
purple-black dust on stamens.

Frustration. No-one around
to share her wonder.

Yet these same poppies in
their garish summer garb,
stopped her in mid-scream.

The old lady in the blue sunhat,
astonished that such
firebrand flowers could be,
gave in to outrageous colour,
sipped her chilled wine ....
for once, *almost* content.

Intimations?

It was nothing really,
a shift in perspective
that's all
my head unloosening
pulling out its stitches,
the spines of books
dipping and spinning
dissolving
into the blue light
of WH Smith, Truro,
and the floor
making waves between
the felt-tip pens and
the 'Well-done' stickers,
the birthday cards for aunties,
the pink and silver cushions
and the red Valentine's hearts
(God, I miss those)
so I made my escape
while the going was good
ignoring
the roll of Sellotape
I'd meant to buy.

I made do with
a packet of Nurofen
from Boots and
two fat bunches of anemones.

Two capsules later,
the books returned
to their shelves,
the pens and pencils

to their proper places,
my head was re-tied
        to my neck,
        (with string this time)
                the anemones exploded
with firework colour
and my seeing eyes
        settled back, safe
                into their sockets.

Washing-up

The dishwasher died in the middle of a cycle,
complete with its load of mugs and cereal bowls.
Like any death, there was a sigh, a loss of movement,
          a sudden silence. I felt its heart –

it was still hot, but had stopped beating.
Just like you. One minute you were talking,
the next pure white stillness. Beyond the doctor's
          skills, you leaked too.

Nor did the dishwasher respond to the repair man's
efforts, so I stood at the sink, hands deep in suds, looking
out over the fields. When you died, I wrote a poem.
          It gave me something to do.

My Mistake

A warm hand on the small of my back –
such a broad sexy hand, a scattering of fine hairs
above the knuckles – signalled his return.
            That and the smell of his skin.

I daren't turn round. He stood behind me, breath
fluttering against my left ear. 'It's me,' he said –
as if I didn't know. And I was happy, relief
            gushing through my body.

How could I have doubted him? Of course
he wasn't dead – I'd been kidding myself
all this time, what with the funeral, winding
            up his affairs, binning his clothes.

My mistake. Except that it wasn't. I woke
alone to a bitter morning, just me and the cat.
It was hard to get up and face the day, his voice
            begging me to believe him.

The Blue Fish

It *was* there, I swear, iridescent
in the light of orange street lamps,
its round black eye following me
as I stepped out of my knickers.

Gift-wrapped, it was, in a silver
foil box, scales in dazzling blues,
from turquoise through to deepest
indigo, a sinister Christmas gift.

I've no idea how it came to lie
on your side of the bed, pulsating
with threat, waiting, just waiting
for me to slide under the duvet.

I tried to stare it down, took time
over the routine of hair-brushing
and hand-creaming, to no avail.
The blue fish was in it to win.

It leered at me as I pulled my
nightdress down over my knees,
knowing somehow I was never
so modest when you were around.

Its ultimate intention, I'm sure,
was the fishy equivalent of a leg-
over. I screwed up enough courage
to throw it into the night, foil and all.

Through a gap in the curtains
its ever-open eye watched me
stumble back to an empty bed
where the pillow still smells of you.

Say It With Flowers

Think of a man
with a rose
in his hand,
a yellow rose,
candle-flame petals
scorching the afternoon.

Think of a man
walking the street,
his bright flower
a torch. See him try
to kindle lovelight
in implacable eyes.

'Don't pester me,'
the woman snaps, turning.
Think of a man
stamping out the ashes
of a flower,
petal by petal.

Camouflage

Poems are the very devil. They
can leap out at you, fully-formed
    on occasion. Mostly
they hide in cracks in the wall,
under flower pots, on the pavement –
    I almost stepped on one,
when I tripped on a drain cover in Bath.

They have a habit of lingering
in once-familiar smells. I'm waiting
    for a poem that started
years ago in my grandmother's kitchen,
but for the life of me, I can't pin it down.

You try to fox them, those recalcitrant
word-strings, jot ideas on the backs of cheque
    books, on shopping lists.
And then you lose them to the supermarket
    trolley, the cat's tray.

They have camouflage that puts the army
to shame, shuffling as they do through
    dreams and nightmares.
So cross your fingers, hold your breath
    and hope for the best.

Poems store their secrets in changing
weather, in lovers' beds, in memories
    of childhood. Breathe out
and, like dandelion heads, they'll disappear.

Space

'I need my space,' the parting
cry from a disillusioned lover –
but space is where we live.

An invisible border, it
outlines our sense of self –
step too close at your peril.

The space inside our skin
is filled with more than
breath and bone and blood.

Imagination hides behind
our eyes, unreels in all its
strangeness to colour poems.

And when we write them
down, spaces are as important
as the words we choose.

The me of me, the you of you
are defined by space – to push away,
to bring close enough to kiss.

Words Sometimes Break …

T S Eliot

I am freaked out by words,
by the sound of them, the way
they lie neatly-packed in
print, bearing no hint
of struggle. They follow
blindly across the page
like a line of ants under
a hot sun. Then they bite.

I am seduced by words. Take
ineffable, its satisfactory
shape, its assonance. Taste
it on the tongue. A perfect
word, infused by the smell
of white roses on a summer
evening. But I wouldn't
dare use it. *Ineffable*
belongs in the head.

I used to think that words
were a game. 'Open it
anywhere, Grandpa,' I'd say.
'Ask me a word.' And I'd
thrust the battered red
Chambers into his hands.
He'd find something suitable
and I'd smirk into action,
loving the welter of words.

And they can have such power.
Words can break and tear and
destroy. Politicians, lovers
and estate agents barter with
them every day. *Inglenook*
fascinates. I see burnished
copper, flowers and firelight –
I would almost buy a house
on the strength of it.

Out Of The Blue

You don't expect an attack dog
to pounce, not this late in the day,
but attack it does, taking ferocious
bites out of your complacency,
carefully carved out of the last
        seven long years.

You discover you still remember
the tart flavour of the man, his
salty skin-smell, the way he asked
for poached eggs, *'two like this ...'*
giving him an excuse to waggle
        two upraised fingers.

You thought you'd come to terms
with things, space in your bed,
the wardrobe, two extra drawers.
It just took four words, *Portsmouth
to St Malo,* for the dogs to be
        unleashed, teeth bared.

Second Coming

Seven poets in jeans and tops, long skirts,
wide-brimmed hats against the sun …
(and not a man among them)
busy, struggling with words,
imperfect images, dialogue,
birthing poems like babies.

Each poet reads aloud, her poems
giving voice to the dead, reinventing them,
putting flesh on bones …
and the men emerge
one by one, jingling
loose coins in their pockets.

They listen, these men, conjured up
in words, *a bare foot, his black shoes,*
unwrinkled morning shirt …
was it really like that?
their bass notes reach
into the corners of the room.

Each man has his moment, Peter
the poet, Allen the accountant, a lost-
and-found lover … like negatives
in the alchemy
of a darkroom, poetry too
has its own brand of sorcery.

Icarus

Sky the colour of a Copper Blue,
Icarus of the summer air, wings
tipping the rim of a ripe sun.
It's a day of anticipation, of silver
sea, of new-sprung leaves. Why
the thirst for what once was?

A Copper Blue can't remember
its carapace, its time in limbo,
Icarus forgets feeding the birds
through prison bars – and his father's
advice – so why *my* memories of
blazing geraniums and that sunhat?

Is it a fattening of poppy buds? Or
the scrape of a butterfly's wing? Is
it magnolia blossom dropping like
melted wax? Whatever it is, it brings
you back, sitting in the sun, (complete
with straw hat), glass of red in hand.

Winter Bird

A winter bird rips up
the four o'clock dark
with jagged song, all
the more rapturous for
its sheer improbability.

On a dreary December
afternoon, against my
better judgment, it jolts
kill-joy memory buds
to open frail white petals.

Of course, it doesn't
last, neither the cut-glass
notes, nor the surge
of unexpected hope, not
now that you've gone.

Tear-jerkers

Windflowers do it, just
by being there, fragile,
brief as snowflakes
scattered in shadow
beneath winter trees.

We used to look out
for them, drawing a blank
time after time. Then,
pinpricks at first, teasing
us. Had they made it?

Before long, a foaming
tide. How could we
have doubted? We'd
turned the corner
of the year yet again.

But that was then. Now
the windflowers flirt
their paper skirts in vain.
I see them. You don't.
Tear-jerkers, every last one.

Powerful Absence

your unseen presence
peers from Post-it notes
   folded in the pages
      of a recipe book
3 heaped egg-spoons
HOT chilli powder –
   if using Spar chilli,
   reduce to 2 level spoons
(to be ignored at one's peril)

hides in little pots
of rescued nails
   among pliers
      brass picture hooks
and Phillips screwdrivers
   in the battered
      blue tool-box

crouches in yellow dust
   from the plastic box
the crematorium people
      gave me
marked, like a school satchel,
      Allen David Jones
(scattered now under Welsh poppies
   where gold petals
      keep you dry in summer rain)

returns in full HD colour
(caught in a branch of the maple tree)
      to tantalise
with a whisper, a smile, a hug
   and a rush of blood
      in now-and-again dreams

Gone, Without Trace

You walked away, that's what
you did. Well, not walked exactly,
more sat down and died.

For a while afterwards
I caught the smell of your scalp
on pillows and cushions, but
like cat-nip, it's been trampled
down, obliterated.

And your voice,
drowned out by wind in the leaves.

If I wake in the night, I roll
across to your side of the bed,
still seeking warmth – shoulder,
belly, chest.
It's a no go, ghosts
are callous, cold and unforgiving.

In my dreams, you do some
really wacky stuff, letting face
and eyes, even your glasses, dissolve
like that Salvador
Dali watch we saw in Paris.

I can't believe the flesh-and-bone
image in our wedding album and holiday
photographs, is really you.

You've thrown a veil of sea-mist
over your features, run for cover
under bright Welsh poppies, flown

into some wild blue yonder far
                                        beyond my ken,
in other words, you've done a bunk.

                                        Gone, without trace.

Indigo Dreams Publishing
132, Hinckley Road
Stoney Stanton
Leicestershire
LE9 4LN
www.indigodreams.co.uk

Papers used by Indigo Dreams are recyclable products made from wood grown in sustainable forests following the guidance of the Forest Stewardship Council.